Control of silica dust in foundries

HS(G)74

GW01458342

CONTENTS

London: HMSO

HS(G) series
The purpose of this series is to provide guidance for those who
have duties under the Health and Safety at Work etc Act 1974
and other relevant legislation. It gives guidance on the practical
application of regulations made under the Act, but it should not
be regarded as an authoratative interpretation of the law.

Enquiries regarding this or any other HSE publications should be
made to HSE Information Centres at the following addresses:

Broad Lane
Sheffield
S3 7HQ
Tel: (0742) 752539
Fax: (0742) 720006

Baynards House
1 Chepstow Place
Westbourne Grove
London
W2 4TF
Tel: (071) 221 0870
Fax: (071) 221 9178

ISBN 0 11 885677 4

INTRODUCTION

1   This advisory booklet has been produced by the Health and Safety Executive's (HSE) Molten Metals National Interest Group to assist the foundries industry in controlling the exposure of its employees to respirable silica dust. It is intended to:

(a) give information about silica in foundry operations;

(b) indicate reasonably practicable means of reducing exposure to silica in these operations; and

(c) highlight the reasons why control measures in foundries typically fail to achieve their purpose.

BACKGROUND

2   Following a review of workers' exposure to silica dust in industry, the Health and Safety Commission's Advisory Committee on Toxic Substances (ACTS), accepted a proposal to:

(a) set a single maximum exposure limit (MEL) of 0.4 mg/m^3 for respirable crystalline silica; and

(b) revoke the existing occupational exposure limits with respect to different forms of crystalline silica ie quartz, cristobalite, tridymite (including flint and similar substances).

3   These changes will come into force on 1 January 1992 and will be accompanied by a general Guidance Note EH 59 *Crystalline silica* and three industry specific, advisory booklets for the foundry, heavy clay and refractory and quarrying industries. Each booklet will deal specifically with conditions in its own particular industry and should be read in conjunction with the general Guidance Note. Other useful references are listed under Further Reading.

EXPOSURE TO SILICA

4   The majority of foundries still use sand as the moulding medium and consequently silica dust will be encountered at many different points throughout the foundry, from sand plants, knockouts and shakeouts to fettling shops and blasting enclosures. In addition to process exposure, there will be other sources such as maintenance and repair, especially of ladles, furnaces and cupolas and general cleaning of floors and plant. Whatever the source, there will be a need to reduce exposure to

silica to as low a level as is reasonably practicable, and in any event, to below the MEL of 0.4 mg/m^3.

TYPICAL EXPOSURE LEVELS

5   The hazards associated with silica have been known for many years and traditionally, local exhaust ventilation and/or respiratory protective equipment have been the preventive measures commonly adopted. Typical exposure levels for some of these operations are as follows:

Knockout/shakeout*	0.04 to 0.38 mg/m^3
Blasting of castings*	0.02 to 0.35 mg/m^3
Furnace lining/re-lining	5.82 mg/m^3 (total dust)
Cupola fettling	50 mg/m^3 (total dust)

* These are measured exposure levels at operations where local exhaust ventilation (LEV) or other engineering controls were fitted and in use. Instances of exposure levels as high as 4.1 mg/m^3 were measured where such controls were either not fitted or not working efficiently.

6   The wide variation in exposure levels is due to a number of factors including:

(a) differing plant and machinery;

(b) silica content of the medium in use;

(c) efficiency of the control measures; and

(d) housekeeping standards.

7   It should be stressed that a high standard of housekeeping will significantly reduce many of the high silica levels measured in foundries.

8   The most common source of silica dust is silica sand and silica in refractories. There is available a limited range of low silica sands. These however, are expensive and are generally used for special applications only. It is unlikely that for the foreseeable future it will be possible to replace silica sand for use as the principal moulding medium.

PROCESS EXPOSURE

Knockout

9   There are three main types of knockout process encountered:

Non-mechanised/manual

10   Castings are separated from their moulds in the open shop in a single position, or in a position which is determined by other work in progress. This can give rise to significant dust and silica levels - the latter often in excess of 0.5 mg/m^3 although usually only for short periods of time.

Figure 1: Knockout in open shop with provision of general, but largely ineffective LEV.

11   In addition to dust arising during knockout, there is often an even greater evolution of dust during manual or mechanical retrieval of sand.

Figure 2: Mechanised retrieval of sand

12   It is recommended that:

(a)   Where possible, the system of work should be modified so as to introduce an element of mechanised knockout, or at least to ensure that all such work is confined to a single, identified area.

(b)   Any area devoted to knockout should be provided with good general ventilation.

(c)   Where high levels of dust and silica are created on a short term basis, appropriate respiratory protective equipment should be provided and worn, even though the time weighted average (TWA) exposure over 8 hours may be below the MEL.

(d) Quantities of sand left on the floor can be transferred by personnel, vehicles and wind thus adding to general background levels throughout the foundry. Sand should, as far as possible, be contained within the assigned knockout area.

(e) Where practicable damp down sand before retrieval is carried out.

Mechanised vibratory

13   Castings are separated from moulds on a vibrating bed or grid. Dust and silica can easily be controlled by side or down draught LEV. The greater the degree of enclosure which can be achieved, the more effective the collection of dust/silica will be. Simple modifications to existing systems such as fitting side enclosures to hoods can greatly improve the performance of equipment by eliminating the interference of draughts. A well designed and maintained system should be able to achieve silica in air levels below 0.1 mg/m^3.

Figure 3: Vibratory knockout with side draft ventilation

Mechanised rotary

14   Castings are separated from moulds by being passed through a rotating drum. Total enclosure can be achieved, thereby enabling a high standard of control of dust and silica.

Figure 4: Rotary knockout with LEV leads to minimal exposure

Fettling

15   Whatever method of fettling is adopted, those castings which are subject to shot blasting first will have a minimal amount of silica still adhering. Any measure designed to control general dust at this process will also provide adequate control over silica. Where shot blasting is not part of the process, then levels as high as 4.0 mg/m^3 can be experienced when working on large castings.

Small/medium castings

16   The fettling method is determined by the size and quality of castings. Castings which are movable either by hand or by lifting and handling systems should be fettled in ventilated booths or enclosures, or should be fettled using equipment which has LEV fitted as an integral part of the system.

Pedestal grinders

17   Pedestal grinders fitted with a recognised LEV system (SCRATA, BCIRA) should give rise to minimal exposure to respirable silica. The system usually consists of exhaust ventilation drawing dust down through a perforated rest and also from the rear of the abrasive wheel guard.

Figure 5: Pedestal grinders fitted with LEV - note the additional use of powered respirators

Cutting off disc/saw

18   Similar systems of LEV to those used for pedestal grinders can be fitted.

19   Levels of control below 0.1 mg/m^3 can be achieved.

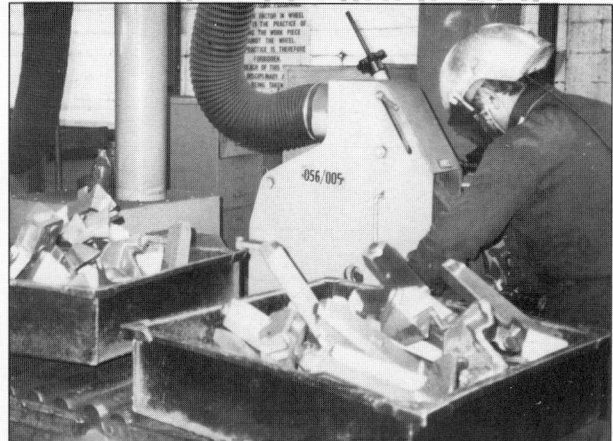

Figure 6: Cutting off discs fitted with LEV

Swing frame grinder

20   By fitting integral flexible extract ventilation ducting from the rear of the grinding wheel through the articulated frame, high standards can be achieved.

Figure 7: Swing frame grinder with LEV

Arc air gouging

21   This process can give rise to high levels of dust and silica. A well designed booth or workroom fitted with extract ventilation should enable control below the occupational exposure limits (OELs) to be achieved.

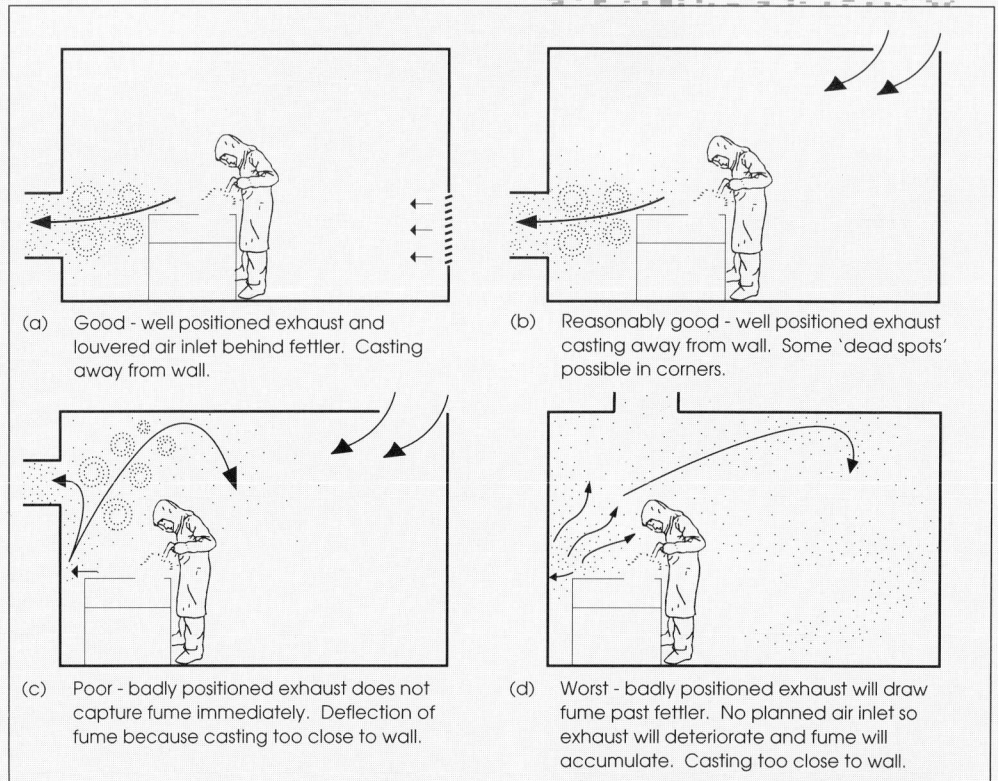

(a)   Good - well positioned exhaust and louvered air inlet behind fettler. Casting away from wall.

(b)   Reasonably good - well positioned exhaust casting away from wall. Some 'dead spots' possible in corners.

(c)   Poor - badly positioned exhaust does not capture fume immediately. Deflection of fume because casting too close to wall.

(d)   Worst - badly positioned exhaust will draw fume past fettler. No planned air inlet so exhaust will deteriorate and fume will accumulate. Casting too close to wall.

Figure 8: Typical booth of arc-air gouging

Hand-held tools

22   A great variety of hand-held tools - angle grinders, chipping hammers, discs etc are used. Well designed, ventilated booths and benches are successful in controlling dust/silica exposure.

Figure 9: Well appointed booth – note that the workpiece is situated close to the rear of the booth

23   Particular attention is required to methods of work adopted. It is important that the workpiece is positioned as close as possible to the extraction points (usually at the rear of the booth). Well designed work benches, or jigs will help, as will appropriate lifting/ handling systems to place the casting.

24   Much of the benefit of LEV will be lost if the operator stands between the extraction system and the casting. The use of turntables will effectively eliminate this problem.

25   As a rough guide, an LEV system achieving a capture velocity of one metre per second (1 m/s) will cope with most dust/silica evolution provided the method of work is suitable.

Automatic

26   There is scope for automating fettling activities. Regular shaped castings lend themselves to this. There are now available CNC systems which can fettle quite complex shapes. Automation enables exhaust ventilation to be fitted to a total enclosure.

Figure 10: Automatic CNC fettling machine

27   It is noticeable in Figures 3, 5, 6, 7 that even where adequate engineering controls exist some operators choose to wear additional protection in the form of powered respirators or simple disposable masks.

Larger castings

28   Some castings will be too large to fit into booths. Large general under floor ventilation systems may help to reduce exposure to dust/silica and some success has been achieved with moveable booths. However, it will normally only be possible to achieve control through the use of appropriate respiratory protective equipment (RPE). Segregation from other operations and regular collection of dust using vacuum systems or wet-brushing is essential in such circumstances.

Figure 11: Fettling large casting using RPE

29   The methods and exposure levels outlined in this section refer to fettling of pre-cleaned castings. Where shot blasting is not carried out, then an assessment of the exposure levels (typically 20 to 30 times higher than for pre-cleaned castings) may indicate the necessity to combine engineering controls with the use of RPE.

Blasting of castings

30   Blasting of castings gives rise to large levels of dust and silica. There are well established techniques for this work, all of which use effective ventilation systems to prevent exposure of operators.

31   All methods of blasting are carried out in enclosures and it is essential that these are regularly checked - even small leaks can give rise to significant general exposure in a work area. The Control of Substances Hazardous to Health (COSHH) Regulations 1988 require monthly thorough examination and tests and these need to be supplemented by daily visual checks.

32   Large castings usually require the shot blasting to be carried out by an operator wearing an air-fed protective helmet within a ventilated enclosure.

33   It is essential that RPE is provided and worn when cleaning down the enclosure since very high levels of dust/silica can occur during this procedure.

Figure 12: Shot blasting equipment

Sand plants

34   A common cause of dust in both sand feed and sand recovery systems is that from spillages due to poorly designed or poorly maintained conveyor systems.

35   All such systems have a designed capacity and excessive loadings will inevitably lead to spillages and damage to the system. These can be reduced by the use of bunkers, or hoppers to control the feed rate.

36   Regular maintenance such as repairs to support rollers, alignment of conveyor belts, replacement of damaged belting and repair of skirts at the base of hoppers and discharge points will reduce general leakage of dust. The use of carefully controlled water sprays will also help, and fully enclosed conveyor systems will minimise the problem.

REPAIR AND MAINTENANCE

Furnace re-lining and cupola fettling

37   Many refractories now contain little or no silica. Where silica is present, very high levels can be created during re-lining and fettling operations. Appropriate use of RPE is the only solution for operators directly engaged in such work. Good general ventilation may be required if other personnel are in the area.

Figure 13: Cupola fettling (note the use of a powered respirator)

Maintenance

38   Control within the MEL can only be assured by ensuring that engineering controls are well maintained and properly used. The harsh regime which often exists in the foundry places a premium on routine checks and maintenance in addition to those statutorily required by the COSHH Regulations.

39   Similarly, where RPE is part of the control measure, then it too, must be subject to routine checks and maintenance.

40   As a guide to assisting with these checks, the following are common faults found in LEV in use in foundries:

(a)   Equipment not switched on.

(b)   Equipment switched on, but the fan controls wrongly wired such that the fan is actually operating in reverse.

(c)   Ducting torn, broken or blocked.

(d)   Filters blocked.

(e)   Inadequate maintenance of booths. Side panels missing or openings not kept closed, resulting in a loss of extraction efficiency.

(f)   Extraneous draughts or the effects from man-cooling fans adversely disturbing the flow of extracted air.

(h)   Poor work methods:

    (i)   work going on too far from or completely
        outside the booth; and

    (ii)   operator interposed between LEV and work piece.

Note: correct use of a dust lamp will quickly and simply identify problem areas.

41   Many of these problems can be attributed to ignorance on the part of managers, supervisors and operators. Knowledge of the operation and limitations of these controls achieved through good training and supervision is an essential part of the control procedure.

HOUSEKEEPING

42   Good housekeeping standards are usually indicative of good control measures. Failure to maintain floors in a clean state can only increase the quantity of dust in air.

43   Regular cleaning should be incorporated into a planned maintenance system both to reduce the dust in air and also as a means of identifying the failure of control systems which lead to spillages etc. Cleaning should be carried out using suitable vacuum equipment, which may be of the portable type or flexible hoses plugged into a ring main. Dry brushing should be prohibited unless no other safe method is available.

RESPIRATORY PROTECTIVE EQUIPMENT (RPE)

44   There may be occasions where the use of respiratory protective equipment (RPE) is likely to be the final option to achieve acceptable long term time-weighted average exposures to respirable crystalline silica. Generally, respiratory protection is of the greatest importance when foundry workers are exposed to high concentrations of dust for short periods of time. Long term exposures to high dust concentrations should be dealt with by other control options suggested within the COSHH Regulations and Approved Code of Practice. Some foundry tasks, most probably relating to fettling and grinding, may produce uncontrolled exposures at moderate levels over a working shift where RPE may be required for longer periods.

45 Assessments of workplace dust concentrations will give an indication of the standard of RPE required. It will always be necessary to provide equipment which is effective against respirable sized particles. The Health and Safety Executive (HSE) guidance booklet *Respiratory protective equipment: a practical guide for users* should be consulted for information on all aspects of selection, training, use and maintenance of RPE.

46 In essence, four types of respirator are most likely to be of benefit in the foundry industry. The lowest form of protection is afforded by disposable filtering face piece respirators and by half mask respirators. A somewhat higher standard of protection may be provided by full-face respirators and by powered respirators with helmets or hoods. HSE's guide on availability of *Respiratory protective equipment: legislative requirements and lists of HSE approved standards and type approved equipment* gives a list of suppliers and manufacturers of RPE who should provide you with all the information needed to make the correct decisions on appropriate selection.

47 The highest dust levels will, in general, require the better standard of RPE protection and it is a sensible decision to choose equipment which will be operating well within its designed capability. Powered respirators will require careful maintenance and recharging facilities if they are to remain effective in use.

48 The key to successful use of RPE is in identifying those tasks and areas where it is needed and establishment of a well defined mandatory respirator policy. Careful use of RPE can result in dramatic reductions in personal exposures and in areas where dust emissions are otherwise uncontrolled, it will be the reasonably practicable option.

49 For a respirator programme to be successful, there are five elements which require careful consideration. Failure in any one of these elements results in loss of protection and exposes operators to a greatly increased risk of developing irreversible and progressive lung conditions in later life. The five elements are:

    (a) selection;

    (b) training;

    (c) use;

    (d) fit; and

    (e) maintenance.

50   **Selection** is in itself a two-stage process relating to performance of the equipment and considerations of the conditions of use. **Training** is a vital component and includes information on how to use the equipment, why it is necessary and when it should be used to gain greatest benefit. The **Use** element relates to knowing when the equipment is required and links in with clear instructions on which part of the plant are mandatory respirator zones. **Fit** relates to ensuring that the operator achieves the essential face seal with the equipment which is absolutely necessary if the suggested level of performance is to be reached. Finally, **Maintenance** and a programme of inspection the equipment ensures that the initial performance characteristics continue throughout the life of the equipment.

51   The use of respiratory protective equipment is not a substitute for proper reasonably practicable control measures but it is an extremely important part of the overall strategy to minimise personal exposures to respirable crystalline silica. Failure to recognise the need for a respirator programme and poor management of the implementation of that programme will result in completely unnecessary operator exposures, which in turn, will lead to greater incidence of unnecessary occupational ill health.

CONCLUSIONS

53   Respirable silica dust can be controlled in the foundry to well below the MEL of 0.4 mg/m^3 provided attention is paid to those details highlighted in this guidance. Provision of appropriate control measures is one part of the exercise but control will only remain effective where there is:

(a) adequate training and supervision; and

(b) an appropriate formal system of checking and maintenance.

FURTHER READING

Regulations

Control of Substances Hazardous to Health Regulations 1988
SI 1988 No 1657 HMSO ISBN 0 11 087657 1

HSE publications available from HMSO

*Control of substances hazardous to health and control of
carcinogenic substances. Control of Substances Hazardous to
Health Regulations 1988. Approved Codes of Practice* L5
(formerly COP29) HMSO 1990 ISBN 0 11 885593 X

Crystalline silica Guidance Note: EH 59 HMSO 1992
ISBN 0 11 8856782

Ventilation of the workplace Guidance Note: EH 22 Rev HMSO
1988 ISBN 0 11 885403 8

Occupational exposure limits 1992 Guidance Note: EH 40/92
HMSO 1992 ISBN 0 11 885696 0

Dust: general principles of protection Guidance Note: EH 44 Rev
HMSO 1991 ISBN 0 11 8855956

An introduction to local exhaust ventilation HS(G)37 HMSO 1987
ISBN 0 11 883954 3

Respiratory protcctivo oquipment: a practical guide for users
HS(G)53 HMSO1990 ISBN 0 11 885522 0

*Respiratory protective equipment: legislative requirements and
lists of HSE approved standards and type approved equipment*
HMSO 1991 ISBN 0 11 885609 X

Silica dust and you MS(A)15 1992. Free from HSE Information
Centres.

HSE Joint Standing Committee on Health, Safety and Welfare in Foundries

COSHH - its application in the foundry HMSO1991
ISBN 0 11 885591 3

*Principles of local exhaust ventilation: first report of the
subcommittee on dust and fume* HMSO 1975 ISBN 0 11 361074 2

*Foundry dust control: fettling benches and small adjustable
hoods: second report of the subcommittee on dust and fume*
HMSO 1975 ISBN 0 11 361077 7

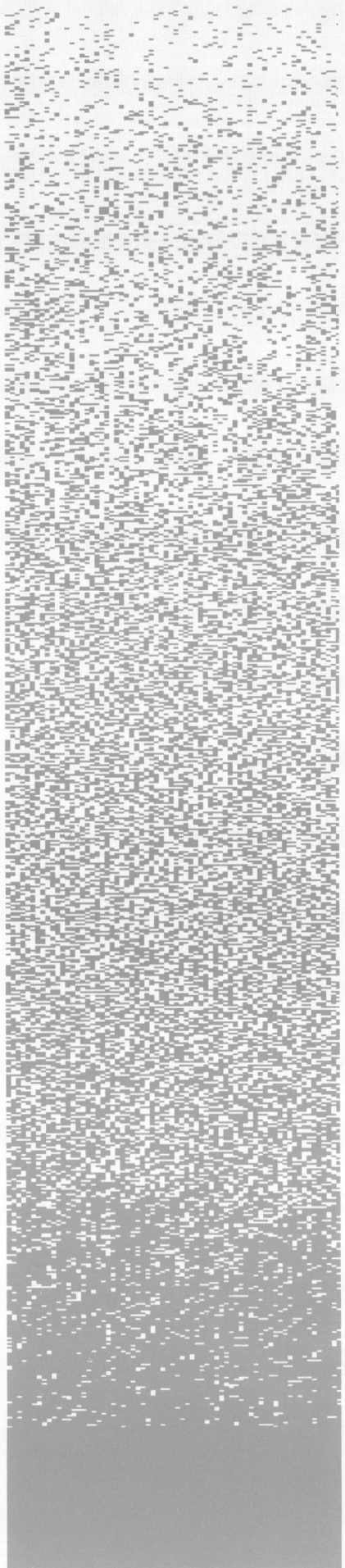

Printed in the UK for HSE, published by HMSO   C40   1/92